PATRICK IRELAND

PATRICK

DRAWINGS 1965-1985

Essay by

with an introduction by

IRELAND

LUCY R. LIPPARD

ELIZABETH BROUN

Published for the National Museum of American Art by the Smithsonian Institution Press   Washington, D.C.   1986

Published on the occasion of an exhibition organized by the
National Museum of American Art, Smithsonian Institution,
Washington, D.C., and shown there April 4–August 17, 1986

Curator for the exhibition: Elizabeth Broun
Photographers: Michael Fischer and Margaret Harmon

Cover: *25 Angled I's on a 5 color 5 x 5 point grid*, 1975
(cat. no. 36)

Library of Congress Cataloging-in-Publication Data:

National Museum of American Art (U.S.)
Patrick Ireland: drawings 1965-1985.

Catalogue of an exhibition organized by the National Museum
of American Art, April 4-August 17, 1986.
Bibliography: p.
Supt. of Docs. no.: SI 6.2:Ir2/965-85
1. Ireland, Patrick—Exhibitions. I. Ireland,
Patrick. II. Lippard, Lucy R. III. Broun, Elizabeth.
IV. Title.
NC139.I73A4   1986   741.973   86-600067

Catalogue design by Stephen Kraft, Washington, D.C.
Text set in Univers by V.I.P. Systems, Inc., Alexandria, Va.
Printed in the United States on Paloma by Schneidereith &
Sons, Baltimore, Md.

The paper used in this publication meets the minimum
requirements of the American National Standard
for Permanence of Paper for Printed Library Materials
Z739.48–1984.

For sale by the Superintendent of Documents
United States Government Printing Office
Washington, D.C. 20402

Contents

cat. no. 43

Foreword

As Minimalism and Conceptualism developed in the 1960s and 1970s, art sometimes seemed to invite commentary almost as a complementary form of content, and the relationship between artists and sympathetic critics grew unusually close. In her essay, Lucy Lippard mentions Patrick Ireland's "curious insider/outsider position" as both artist and critic in the small circle evolving these new ideas. Many people are aware of Ireland's role as an outsider—as a critic writing under the name of Brian O'Doherty for *Artform* and the *New York Times* and as editor of *Art in America*. As an insider, though, Ireland's contribution is less well known, although his art was often on the cutting edge and his give-and-take with colleagues like Eva Hesse, Don Graham, Robert Smithson, Sol LeWitt, Mel Bochner, Peter Hutchinson, and others was salt to the broth. There was an exhilarating atmosphere of shared invention and discovery for several years, before artists migrated into more private spheres where ideas that had germinated earlier grew in different directions. For Ireland, perceptual theories first explored in the 1960s became the focus of a considerable body of work continuing to the present day.

The exhibition *Patrick Ireland: Drawings 1965–1985* is designed to bring this insider's work to the fore by showing his considerable achievements as an artist. Necessarily many chapters of his career have been omitted; this exhibition does not include his sculptures and his installations can be documented only through drawings, and in some cases, no record exists. The drawings assembled here, however, demonstrate Ireland's rich thinking about perception and language over a twenty-year period.

Our deepest thanks go to Patrick Ireland for his gracious cooperation and goodwill throughout the project, to Lucy Lippard for her splendid essay, and to the Department of Foreign Affairs in Dublin for a generous contribution to the catalogue. Chief Curator Elizabeth Broun conceived and ably coordinated this special exhibition, drawing upon the excellent assistance of Margy Sharpe, Patricia Geeson, Melissa Kroning, and Mary Kaye Gwiazdowski of the museum staff who coordinated the loans and photography; Judith Brodie of the National Gallery of Art staff also provided assistance. The catalogue was edited by Migs Grove and produced by the Smithsonian Institution Press for the museum. A special thanks is due to James Volkert and Allan Kaneshiro and the museum's installation staff for their work on the installation.

Charles C. Eldredge
Director

Patrick Ireland from A to I

ELIZABETH BROUN

Patrick Ireland's drawings offer a surprisingly clear avenue into the work of this elusive and paradoxical artist. He prefers not to "curate his own career" and so has been casual about keeping track of early paintings from the 1950s and his sculptures from the 1960s. His art entered a world full of Duchampian skepticism about the status of the art object and the claim of history on the present and future. Subverting both history and the object, Ireland has, since the early 1970s, granted his major projects only the brief life span of a temporary installation, which leaves no relic to be sold or collected, apart from the drawings that mark the event. About the same time, he changed the name under which he exhibited, a move that complicated the matter of public reputation but also denied the role of autobiography in his art. He effectively eliminated both the object and the artist from the work— a risky approach, but one that concentrated attention on the idea, since there was nowhere else for attention to go.

Ideas pared to essentials often take the form of line. For twenty years, Ireland has made drawings as notebook jottings, studies for sculptures or installations, documents of completed projects, or independent artworks, together forming the most complete available evidence of his continuously evolving investigations. Whether drawn with watercolor marker, scratched in steel, or delineated by a stretched rope, Ireland's art is inherently graphic in that it always pulls toward the irreducible; levels of reality collapse into a single thin line (the extension of a point), just as matter collapses into a black hole.

Ireland's line never attempts description or illusion, nor is it autographic or expressive. His work comes closest to the act of mapping in that it plots a conceptual space and proposes hypothetical movements based on constructed systems. The paths traced by his line incorporate notions of time and duration, origin and destination, changing points of perception, direction, and reversibility. In the Rope Drawings, space is a raw material, a *terra incognita* temporarily structured by the rope that provides landmarks for those who walk through it. Just as water parts for a ship and engulfs the space vacated by its passage, the "wilderness" (as Ireland calls it) of amorphous space yields briefly to Ireland's will before reverting to its undifferentiated, essentially unknowable state. Time and language are similar to space in that they too are easily degradable media, tending toward entropy unless energized by a structure or system, which for Ireland is best conveyed through graphic means. Like Klee or Steinberg, who also balanced their thoughts on a line, Ireland cares nothing for draftsmanship per se; line simply comes to the rescue when ideas collide.

The earliest drawings here, from 1965–68, are determined to remain *work* rather than artwork. Ground plans, cross sections, and isometric views fill some sheets, arranged in conflicting orientations in a curious minimalist *horror-vacui*. Cheap graph paper, smudges, fingerprints, erasures, and tape stains testify to Ireland's disdain of craft and insistence on refining the ideas rather than the object. The autographic quality of drawing is consistently ignored, once even eliminated in favor of the typewriter. Notions of quality in materials or draftsmanship are dismissed almost as a form of consumerism or vanity. A seriousness of purpose comes across clearly, as well as an urgency and excitement about the ideas. The autographic quality of drawing is consistently ignored, eliminated in favor of the typewriter or an electrocardiograph.

Color and composition are introduced gradually for functional rather than decorative purposes. The five vowels appear as five colors, and grids or magic squares impose a compositional logic on the sheet. Little by little color and composition begin to assert their own allure, which Ireland seems first to have tolerated and then enjoyed but not encouraged. The beauty of paper or watercolor coexists with the concepts these materials were summoned to express, and the eye is granted a few rights but never given first consideration. The visual shimmer of some of the 1970s drawings is the more startling because it is a "found" quality in the work, a lyricism Ireland hadn't looked for and didn't want to exploit. In some of the Vowel and Image/Afterimage Drawings, he slices lines still thinner and shrinks dots to pinpoints so the eye must turn to a higher power of concentration, restoring the balance between seeing and perception.

Ireland generally works in series, each series investigating one or more of the artificial constructs that shape perception and experience. Language, time, space, and sensory experience all depend on such armatures, for which Ireland finds graphic equivalents: the Ogham Drawings use serial linear notation to mediate between language and perception; the Vowel Drawings derived from Ogham reflect the infinite permutations of these primal sounds; the Rope Drawings anchor space with a line that offers both "favored" vantage points and constantly shifting relationships. Ireland shows little interest in the traditional artist's concern for nature, the studio, characterization, autobiography, media, or issues of composition and form. He's searching in these drawings for a way of making our perceptual "windows on the world" less transparent, so they can be understood as the veils and mirrors they really are.

Certain drawings seem to summarize Ireland's explorations of perceptual systems. It's as if he wants to put all the systems into a single drawing to emphasize that each is fully arbitrary and constructed, merely a viewpoint on experience. *The Five Senses of the Bishop of Cloyne* condensed his interest in the senses, numerical relationships, color codes, and magic squares and marked his move into language systems and the Celtic Ogham alphabet. The drawing is almost impenetrably dense with information, and few will "read" it to the end, although it synopsizes Ireland's period of greatest discovery. Composed in serial fashion in rows across the sheet, one system factors into another like a mathematical problem with constantly changing variables. A later drawing is more synthetic; *Angled Vowels at Three Scales* layers the systems rather than stringing them out, so the three sizes of vowels appear against a ground of dots arranged in an implied grid,

The Five Senses of the Bishop of Cloyne
pg. 32

Angled Vowels at Three Scales
pg. 42

which is based on numerical relationships derived from Ogham! The effect is richly contrapuntal as the mind juggles all systems simultaneously, but finally so many layered networks lessen rather than increase our confidence that experience can be caught in even the finest mesh. The more places that Ireland sets his traps for experience, the more he shows that it can't be held. The beauty of this drawing is not that it captures an aspect of reality, but that it shows the many clever strategies of the mind at work— a visual evocation of that background hum called consciousness.

Just as his drawings often produce an unexpected lyricism, the leitmotif of perceptual systems is somehow shadowed by skepticism and doubt, which is equally unexpected. The minimalist clarification of intellectual constructs somewhere intersects with a neomedieval scholasticism, full of paradoxes, as when Ireland lays out all possible permutations of the indivisible word One, or projects the infinitely variable forms of the Ogham spelling of I, or shows the exquisite neutrality of the indefinite article A. Wittgenstein, William of Occam, and Bishop Berkeley make cameo appearances in some drawings, but the distrust of the senses and the mirage world they create goes past philosophical teaching and eventually circles back on what one writer has called Ireland's "skirmishes with identity."

In a curious way this art restates the discoveries of modern physics, which also holds that there is no objective reality independent of the observer, that measuring one aspect of a particle absolutely precludes knowing other aspects of the same particle; that randomness precludes certainty or prediction; that matter and energy are interchangeable; that "reality" is formed of discontinuous units rather than solid substance. If Ireland seems in search of a "unified field theory"—an Absolute that would embrace ONE HERE NOW—it is not because he is either a romantic in love with chaos or a classicist discovering an orderly universe, but a skeptic who sees order and chaos, progress and stagnancy, A and I, as obverse and reverse of a coin.

Ireland's Dot Drawings reconcile several dialectical extremes. They are both figure and ground, drawing and pointillist tone, grid and field, system and freedom. The scatter effect seems to keep all the dots in motion—"quanta" bouncing with various velocities off the walls of the grid, which in the later work is usually implied (left blank) rather than drawn. Ironically, the method Ireland devised to ensure that the dots would look random is almost impossible for anyone else to master, so when he uses assistants to make dotted wall drawings, individual "hands" appear like fingerprints. This difficulty in escaping a pattern is a kind of metaphor for our habit of imposing shape on experience or perception.

Ireland's approach to the Dot Drawings begins in system and clarity and ends in obsession bordering on the mystical. Densities of the dot fields are established by mathematical ratios; the artist then "logs" the multiples of hundreds or thousands of dots by making small dot notations in the margin of the sheet, as if counting beads. What other artist deals in infinite repetition of the smallest act of drawing? Ireland has much in common with the master of the *Book of Kells*, who also began with the Word and whose governing compositional device—the cross—also described a grid. Both artists first choose a system and then submit to it, a form of abnegation of the self—a self that is, perhaps, merely a pattern imposed on a field, another constructed system.

While raising all these issues, Ireland's drawings alone cannot convey his fullest exploration of them, for much of his work was conceived as sculpture, performance, or installation that involve the viewer in an active way. One surprising result of seeing the paper works assembled as a group is to realize the gift he has for turning drawing into metaphor. If modern physicists find one drawback of the new theory to be that it cannot be visualized like a classical Newtonian clockwork, Ireland has found a means of giving graphic form to the perplexing, even disturbing questions that confound us still.

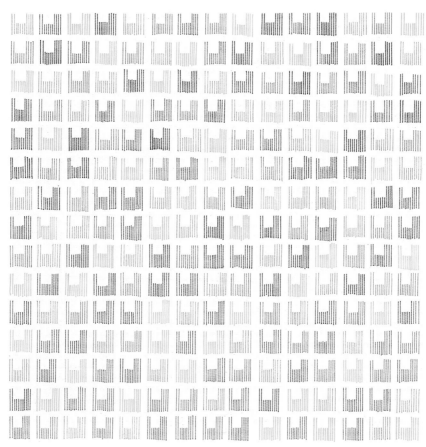

cat. no. 18

ONE HERE NOW

LUCY R. LIPPARD

In art, it is not the absolute relationships that are decisive, but those arbitrary relationships within a system of images dictated by the particular work of art.
—Sergei Eisenstein

Forms, colors, densities, odors—what is in me that corresponds with them? —Walt Whitman

The past serves only to become acquainted with actuality. But actuality escapes me. What, then, is actuality? —Henri Focillon

A slippery thread of ambivalence runs through Patrick Ireland's outwardly serene work. His art is about the senses, but it is neither sensual nor sensuous; it is antihistorical, and yet deeply concerned with time and memory; it is based on systems and seems to elude them; it is insistently modest, temporary, and finite, but indirectly confronts immortality and infinity.

Patrick Ireland (né and aka Brian O'Doherty) was raised in a small Irish town. In the early 1950s he studied art and medicine simultaneously, showing paintings in Dublin and London while in medical school. He has since been a researcher, television host, art critic, and arts administrator as well as an artist. In 1972, with a ritual performance in Dublin he changed his "artist's name" (like a magic name in primitive societies) to Patrick Ireland, "until the British military presence is removed from Northern Ireland and all citizens are granted their civil rights."

Ireland began showing steadily in New York in the mid-sixties and held a curious insider/out-sider position within the Minimal/Conceptual movements as commentator, supporter, intelligent critic, and participant. As his own serial work was just developing, Ireland described the contrary platforms of many of his minimalist colleagues:

If art is about revolution, avoid even counterrevolution. If art is about invention, avoid invention by camouflaging it in apparent simplicity. If art history is about development, avoid development and subvert scholarship. There are no problems. Systems fall apart into their components; it is as if all the integers that went into the common denominator had risen above the line.[1]

This statement is interesting not only for the ways in which it illuminates others' work (Robert Smithson, Sol LeWitt, and Dan Graham were those with whom Ireland had most in common), but for its line/number imagery. Ireland's serial work came into its own with a synthesis of two "autobiographical" components: first, experimental psychology research in Cambridge, England, on the senses—the ways in which the categories of recognition are broken and reformulated in the process of perceiving change; second, his rediscovery of Ogham—the linear, serial translation of the Roman alphabet by Irish Celts around the fourth to fifth centuries A.D.

A 1966 drawing in blues and grays—*Study for the Five Senses: Hearing*—represents the pre-Ogham stage of Ireland's search for a visual system of the senses. It is a study for a columnar sculpture within which a series of motorized clay

Study for the Five Senses: Hearing
pg. 31

reliefs move past viewing windows. The reliefs show the fetus in an early stage, a later stage, then the ear as it develops before birth, ending with a tri-lobed, planar form—the canals that determine spatial orientation.

For all the apparent simplicity and order of Ireland's art, and its scientific underpinnings, the middle ground is somehow precarious. There are pulls in the directions of both Dada and Constructivism. In 1968 he wrote that Hans Richter, a fellow serial artist whose 1920s films impressed him, was "able to maintain relationships with both poles of modernism, both socially and within his own psyche."[2] Similarly, Ireland, who calls himself a "Tatlin man" (as opposed to a Malevich man),[3] is no purist. Although he uses what he calls a "model T form of esthetics," irrationality slides through the interstices of his logical structures, illustrating LeWitt's dictum: "Conceptual artists are mystics rather than rationalists. They leap to conclusions that logic cannot reach."[4]

A certain perversity (the soul of wit) informs Ireland's entire oeuvre. In 1966, for instance, he recognized the Dada of them all when he made a "found" portrait of Marcel Duchamp by recording his electrocardiograph. Duchamp agreed to sit (or lie) for his portrait if Ireland promised to sign it "M.D." The resulting series of drawings centers on a fake oscilloscope in which the master's heart beats on and on, offering a kind of immortality, playing on permanence and impermanence, and ironically paralleling Duchamp's own secret life insurance—the monumental tableau on which he had secretly been working for

years after publicly stating that he had given up art. The cardiograph drawings focus on a T-wave that is the heart's "lead" (as in leading man or follow the leader, recalling mythical journeys and the "tracks" of Ireland's drawings, in which the viewer must follow the dots and lines to a collaborative conclusion with the artist). One of the Duchamp portrait constructions is lighthoused, appropriately, in a found frame—a carpenter's "spirit level."

This was a complex work, and a rather audacious one, challenging as it did the life and work of a veritable myth. Although the two never talked about art, Ireland saw the piece as a dialogue with Duchamp in which he borrowed from him a vital faculty and hung it on the wall, proving that art on the wall was not yet dead. One of the three boxes slowed the heartbeat; the second added up all the heartbeats of a lifetime; this number was then divided by the slowed number per minute, which equalled twenty, and resulted in a five-time extension of Duchamp's lifetime—a "cruel" gesture, Ireland suggests, in that it forced him to begin life over. The mythical journey ends in compulsory rebirth.

At the time that he "discovered" Ogham, Ireland had been riffling through history looking for the right visual armature for his ideas about perception. He had systematically perused Mayan calendars (in Mayan the word *dzib* means both writing and drawing), hieroglyphs, runes, Asian and Arabic writing, and early mathematical notations. Finally he came across Ogham—"the only perfect serial language among ancient modes of signification. . . . You learn this as a kid in

Ireland, but I'd forgotten about it. . . . There it was in the backyard all the time."[5]

Ogham is a linear system of one to five strokes in four permutations: vertical lines cross a horizontal line (or an edge or corner, when carved on stone pillars), stand above the "lintel," hang below it, or are slanted across it. Ogham was the heir to much older alphabets that go back to numbers counted on fingers and trees, which in turn go back to the times when the magic of regularity began to replace random knowledge of the world. With order came the chaos of new possibilities, or permutations, and choices, and new mysteries. Ireland's drawings are, in another turn, heir to these.

The standing stones on which Ogham was carved were, appropriately, boundary markers and perhaps astronomical markers. It was not, however, the stones or their romantic contexts that interested Ireland, but the complexities of this apparently simple system. Unlike the rooted pillar, or the ambiguously reflective rods of Ireland's sculptural work, the line alone implies motion, direction, connections, vortices. Ogham offered Ireland an instrument, or a toy, like James Joyce's puns, free of everything but their roots; or like Samuel Beckett's gray games, the counting of stones, the reciting of hopeless charms.

Ogham also enabled Ireland to escape the literary in art, which haunts the Irish. Visually and substantially, Ogham has more in common with musical notation, and Ireland was, in fact, much impressed in the 1960s by composer Morton Feldman's concepts of an auditory plane, the possibility of "thinking horizontally, and ver-

tically, and obliquely at the same time."[6] With Ogham, Ireland could "split words *and* letters open, explode them into phonemes and morphemes as verbal meaning was regressed into a kind of visual redundancy."[7] (But he also recalls Gertrude Stein's distinction between insistence and repetition.)

As a visual artist, Ireland is more interested in the alphabet than in the language itself. Translating Roman letters (which looked "too interesting") into lines avoided "free rides from linguistics" and offered a new flexibility: "You can read them up and down, right and left, in reflection and reflected again."[8] Ireland's drawings, in fact, recall the photographs of reflections he made in the mid-sixties, collecting ideas then applied to his shining metal columns in which the surfaces functioned as both space and solid—a topological image of inside and outside simultaneously. Mirroring, a metaphor for variety within sameness, symmetry and asymmetry, has generated much of his art.

A key drawing from 1967–68 demonstrates the transition from conceptual illustration to the full-fledged idea that has since fueled twenty years of work. *The Five Senses of the Bishop of Cloyne*[9] is a key in several senses—to the period in which Ireland unlocked Ogham as a stimulatory medium and to the oeuvre itself. Three magic squares picture finger, ear, tongue, nose, and eye—different sense ratios applied to different objects. First they are drawn, then overlaid with color, then they vanish, leaving only a grid of color. The medium between the pictures and the Ogham translations below are three

The Five Senses of the Bishop of Cloyne
pg. 32

mathematical equations and the linear alphabet translated into ours. A key at the top assigns each sense organ a descending series of five numerals with five as the interval—eye: 5, 10, 15, 20, 25; ear: 4, 9, 14, 19, 24; nose: 3, 8, 13, 18, 23; finger: 2, 7, 12, 17, 22; tongue: 1, 6, 11, 16, 21—so that each sense has five different "powers" of description. The Ogham alphabet then spells out the sensations on the left, and the lack thereof on the right—where the words *invisible, impalpable, odorless, tasteless, soundless* result in a void.

Soon after Ireland began to develop his serial ideas around the Ogham alphabet, the vowels began to dominate, perhaps as part of a decision to work on contradictory and trembling ground—not only between word and image, but between "primitive" and modernist. The vowels are primal, fluid sounds that must have originated before the staccato consonants, as the seas mythically came before the land that gave them form and as time flowed before history marked it. Seriality itself is a fluid conception. Ireland's focus on the vowel I and the number One also reflects an attraction to origins.

The vowels are numerically translated in Ireland's drawings: A = 1; O = 2; U = 3; E = 4; I = 5. The grid is often fifteen squares because $1 + 2 + 3 + 4 + 5 = 15$, and the I-Drawings are all based on five. ONE is more complex: an Ogham O is two verticals through the horizontal; N is four verticals hanging from a horizontal "lintel"; E is four verticals crossing the horizontal. Ireland also orchestrated the permutations of ONE (ONE, NEO, EON, OEN, ENO(S), NOE(L)—or unity, nov-elty, time, wine, man, festival) and spelled out in Ogham the ultimate existential statement: ONE HERE NOW.

Literally translated into Ogham and then turned loose into any number of permutations, this system engendered series after series. In the late 1960s/early 1970s, color was added to the linear element, taking off from the idea (but not the specifics) of Rimbaud's sonnet *Voyelles*, possibly inspired by the colors in the primer from which the poet learned to read.

The addition of color permitted Ireland to "spread the sensorium over language, to maximize mobility, but remain firm." The notion of concretizing and syncretizing the senses and physical experience, such as geographical directions and seasons, has been attractive through the ages. Yet color systems in modern aesthetics are classic examples of the subjective masquerading as the objective. Ireland's use of color—"descriptive rather than esthetic"—is arbitrary. A different chromatic system, or lack of one, is assigned to one drawing or one series or one part of a drawing. Sometimes the use of color will change or progress within a drawing, serving to make the lines and vowels more *dense* as things in themselves. Perceptual intensity and diffusion is the goal rather than systemic consistency.

The early Ogham Drawings remained faithful to that particular alphabet—straight lines over and under the horizontal—though rotating and "writing" with it. The rows of lines integrated systemic firmness and formal delicacy, capturing the best of both worlds. The framework is often provided by the magic square—a "nice little machine [that] adds up" diagonally, horizontally, vertically, or all three. The magic square represents perfection as a starting point and offers the artist a "cat's cradle of relationships" as well as a sympathetic form—the grid with which the artists of the late sixties were so enamored because it was a "neutral" field on which to play sensuous or cerebral games without creating traditional forms.

Ireland's art balances between sensing and sensed, and by using the alphabet rather than the language, he emphasizes the channel through which communication occurs. The artwork becomes a vehicle for perception rather than a thing in itself, and the artist simply becomes the executor of the system's desires. Paralleling Sol LeWitt's much quoted statement that the idea is the machine that generates the artwork, Ireland saw his "inside/outside dialectic generating all sorts of phony engines pushing fiction, ideas." He was greatly relieved when he got to the point where understanding his art had nothing to do with him personally—an illusion, surely, but one that has clearly aided him in his art making.

"Memory for me is about the present," he has said. By working with temporary installations and with drawings that challenge memory in themselves, he courts the present as a way of evading posterity and "buying my freedom from the art game." On the other hand, the viewer's memory of Ireland's art must also coexist with his or her chronological, spatial, and personal vortices of remembering. One of the foundations of this work is the idea of "perceptual choice"—conventionally illustrated by the textbook drawing of two facing profiles (black on white) that become a vase (white on black), depending on the viewer's directed perception. Ireland's drawings lead the viewer through a labyrinth of conceptual and perceptual contexts, laying systems over systems over systems. If you look at one of his Vowel Drawings with one idea in mind, you might find it; with another, another—the patterns changing under differing stimuli. Indeterminacy invites, even demands, resolution by our own choice. Hal Foster accurately described the labyrinthine experience of Ireland's oeuvre when he said of the rope drawing *Borromini's Portal*: "We become less aware of unity than of unity's illusion."[10]

In the seventies, Ireland freed his vowels from the Ogham horizon. They flew into gridded or open space, often not touching each other. They never touched the sides of their rectangular containers because that would be "too European," i.e., would make closed, related, geometric forms within a form. In many of these drawings the lines are actually "strokes," *touching* or touching down on the surface void. In others, all the lines touch and form new wholes with, instead of within, the frame. The I-Drawings took fives through an amazing array of relationships. Five straight equal lines might become a sedate field of identical lines differentiated by weight or color, an exuberant field of five-legged zigzags, a grid of changing intervals, a paced frame around a void, or a "Mondrian" in which the size and shape of interlocking rectangles are established by the familiar number systems.

During the seventies, the lines were also overlaid with or defined in absentia by dots. Colors, scales, intervals, systems, and codes were combined, synthesized, juxtaposed, and superimposed. The process has been cumulative and amazingly fertile. One series of fives consisted of wiggly, threadlike lines falling over each other in almost humorous patterns. A later variation of wobbly colored strokes on raw canvas was executed by dropping a hair on the surface and tracing its enlarged trajectories—shades of Duchamp's *Standard Stoppages*. Another bow to history is a 1977 drawing titled *For Malevich, Even Though . . .*, a yellow-dotted reference to the Russian's *Yellow Quadrilateral on White* of 1918.

Another series dealt more conventionally with perception, exploring image/afterimage ratios of intensity in colored dots set in a circle, or wheel, and tonal "aerial perspectives." Some related to the rotational aspect of the Bride's (or Saint Brigid's) Cross—a kind of cartwheel related to the ancient swastika, or sun sign, that can generate an infinite system: "It's very simple, but once you lost the idea, you'd be lost."

"The setting of the system is the key," says Ireland. "Too tight and everything freezes; too loose, and who cares." His systems are preconditions to the actual experience that he hopes the viewer will carry away in memory. Once one is familiar with these systems, it's fun to try and read the drawings without consulting a key. (Even the artist can't always do it.) Though they are not intended as puzzles, it only seems fair that the viewer be able to play too—*play* in Otto

Rank's sense, in order to diminish fear of destiny and liberate creative, life-giving energy.

All games have rules, however, and this is an area where Ireland's relationship to the systems with which he constructs his drawings becomes a dialectic. While acknowledging that "sensations don't lie, but interpretations do, and *will*," Ireland is also interested in the controls, or prohibitions, imposed on a system. The ancient Gaelic concept of *fé geasa* (under restriction) creates characters fated to perform certain acts or act in certain ways, like the stylized predetermined movements of chess pieces. The rules of a game are a "perfectly logical construct that in process generates the unexpected. All games are systems with enough freedom to invoke change, which in turn is courted by skill." Ireland quotes Louis Pasteur: ". . . chance favors only the mind that is prepared," and Branch Rickey: "Luck is the residue of design."

There is an element of drama in Ireland's art making and, faithful to the Irish oral tradition, he has recognized this by performing or directing "readings" of the Vowel Drawings. *Vowel Chorus for Five Voices* is soon to be recorded: "I haven't any idea how it will sound," he says, "but I trust its structure to make itself felt through the caterwauling." He has choreographed and scored his drawings' systems as Structural Plays, in which the actors (performing in minimal costume on a gridded floor) become those legendary characters—the alphabet—and are *fé geasa*. Changes are rung on simple sentences with vocal emphasis as the medium: "OPEN the door" having an entirely different meaning from "Open

Vowel Chorus for Five Voices
pg. 37

THE door'' or ''Open the DOOR.'' And from each visually identical sentence, a whole new web of possibilities emerges.

In the last few years, Ireland's drawings have become more centralized, their open systems have drawn into themselves. After weaving a mesh of many systems in the mid-seventies, he began to complicate the process further by introducing planes in space—cubes and open boxes defined by dots, lines, and a new element—an unruled crosshatching that gives a gauzy effect and permits a chromatic density rarely attained before. Sometimes cubes are dissected into linear Z-forms, implying both two- and three-dimensional planes, which in turn became open boxes with flying flaps. When ''slammed shut,'' they may or may not meet in perfect union. They are visual puns, continuing to form new gestalts through perception itself.

While the alphabetical/numerical components may be harder to discern in the recent work, they are still there, and often read HCE—Here Comes Everybody, or Humphrey Chimpden Earwicker, from *Finnegan's Wake*. The letters appeared in real space in the 1985 *Purgatory (Rope Drawing #74)* at Trinity College in Dublin. In many of the Rope Drawings, however, spatial relations have completely replaced language.

The Rope Drawings are beyond the scope of this essay, but since several drawings for them are included in the exhibition, some parallels should be noted. Like the drawings on paper (and occasionally on canvas), the rope pieces are participatory, offering perceptual options and even entertainments. Where the paper drawings demand movement in the mind's eye, the Rope Drawings demand physical movement, comparable to the thought processes that formed them. You as viewer can even choose not to take your designated place—the vantage point where the piece is perceptually completed. You can subvert the artist's intentions by moving around, *and* you can be seduced into the spot where it all comes together—the point of psychological satisfaction, of outwitting displacement, of focusing the lines and walls, of having *found your place* (ONE HERE NOW). Like concentration on the systems of the paper drawings, the process brings the pleasure of understanding, or the illusion of comprehension. ''Dealing with a given space is a quasi-social act,'' said Ireland in 1980. ''I'm not making art for the ages, I'm making art in one place for a limited time for whatever community I can find there. The gallery is placeless by definition. If the piece is successful, people come in and make a place out of it.''[11]

Antihistorical, antiromantic, antimetaphorical, Ireland is nevertheless creating his own mysteries, divulged to the viewer across time, space, surface, process. He has set himself a modest task, and a valuable one, which in no way protects him against the desire to be understood. Ireland admired Ad Reinhardt's retrospective at the Jewish Museum in 1967 (row after row of ''identical'' black paintings) because ''time as a development was shown to be artificial.'' Looking for what he can't find (as opposed to not being able to find what he's looking for), Ireland hopes to avoid the ''egotism of history.''

Purgatory (Rope Drawing #74) pg. 56–57

Ireland occupies a curious place between the perceptual and conceptual positions staked out in the 1960s (now blurred beyond recognition outside of individual oeuvres). Unlike LeWitt, whose work his outwardly resembles, Ireland is less concerned with the printouts of his generative systems than with the ways in which the senses enrich and simultaneously betray experience. He is less interested in communication than in "forms of communion."[12]

As a writer and an artist, Ireland ambivalently believes that "there is a deep antagonism between word and image. Insofar as a society is preliterate, it weights its images heavier in the scale of its social transactions. When the written word dominates, art is worn away by the endless drip-drip-drip of words."[13] The words buried in his art, then, are elemental, and barely separated from sound and glyph, still mixed with number in a primal relationship. He rejects the systemic consistency of some of his colleagues because it separates eye and mind, preferring his own arbitrary aesthetic choices *within* a system as a way to integrate the two. He does not acknowledge the separation between perceiver and perceived, or at least "asks questions about that separation. Do we become what we look at? What is me and what isn't me? It gets back to a very primitive question of boundaries that are the first element of self-recognition."[14]

"I'm beginning to think the dialectic of this period may be perception and mythology," said Ireland at a panel in 1976. "It's difficult and dangerous to put the two together."[15] That was a time when a great many North American artists were mining ancient cultures and prehistory for ideas and images that would put them back into contact with forces of belief and nature lacking in today's alienated society. Eire, with its melancholy, magical aura, provided a rich lore, and the Celtic heritage of a misty twilight world of "betweenness," neither here nor there, then nor now, allusive and elusive, has become something of a stereotype, particularly problematic for contemporary Irish artists.

"I was surrounded by the labyrinth idea as a kid, in Ireland, where you never get straight answers, you always get bent answers. Partly as reaction, I suppose, I was very strong on concrete things and ideas."[16] In fact, Ireland got his revenge by straightening out labyrinth plans, such as that of Hampton Court, by representing right and left turns and their relationships to the whole in straight parallel lines. For a labyrinth show at Finch College in 1967, he also contradicted the form's inherent mystery by making his piece very simple, easy to read, and in addition, so low that if you walked through it you had a clear overview at all times; you always knew where you were instead of getting lost and then found. In mythical terms, you did not go back to the womb to be reborn, but subverted the unconscious by consciously controlling the process.

Ireland subscribes to Bishop Berkeley's idea that what we perceive exists only in our minds. Sounding very Irish indeed, he admits,

I don't trust the world, or more truly my senses, and I think there is always considerable doubt that the world exists. It may be common among Irish people that the world is not really as it looks. . . . There's a rural saying in Ireland: "Where is the center of the world?" The answer is "Where I'm standing" [ONE HERE NOW]. . . . I've never been convinced of that distinction between inside and what's out there . . . that division always seems to me very threatening. The most difficult ground is the middle ground.[17]

And despite the yearning of a circuitous mind for the straight path, that middle ground is where Patrick Ireland works.

Notes

Unless otherwise noted, quotations come from the artist—from conversations with and letters to the author—or from the following writings and interviews.

1. "Minus Plato," *Art and Artists* (September 1966); reprinted in Gregory Battcock, ed., *Minimal Art* (New York: E.P. Dutton, 1968), 251–55.

2. *Hans Richter* (New York: Byron Gallery, 1968), catalogue text. Ireland made the scenario for a Richterian film called *Black* in 1967 and shared with Richter his affinities for music.

3. One of Tatlin's first Painting Reliefs, *The Bottle* (1913), analyzes the shape through reflection and two- and three-dimensional puns, reminiscent of some of Ireland's metal structures. Tatlin's conclusion that "the most esthetic forms are the most economical" might also appeal to Ireland.

4. Sol LeWitt, "Sentences on Conceptual Art," *0-9* (New York, 1969).

5. Elayne Varian, "Interview with Brian O'Doherty," *Art International* 14 (December 1970): 31–33.

6. *Ibid.*

7. "Wordless Images/Imaged Words," *Poetry East* 13/14 (Spring/Summer 1984): 164–66.

8. Varian, *Art International*.

9. Bishop George Berkeley, 1685–1753 (who was also born in Ireland and lived for a while in colonial America), wrote that objects of perception exist only in the mind.

10. Hal Foster, "Patrick Ireland," *Artforum* (November 1980), 84.

11. John Coplans, "Extracts from a Conversation Between John Coplans and Patrick Ireland," *Dialogue* (Akron Art Institute, 1980).

12. Varian, *Art International*.

13. "Wordless Images/Imaged Words," *Poetry East*.

14. Coplans, "Extracts from a Conversation."

15. "A Symposium," *Projects for PCA* (Philadelphia College of Art, 1976), 32.

16. "Janet Kardon Interviews Some Modern Mazemakers," *Art International* (April–May 1976), 64–68. Ireland also did some flat labyrinths on mirrors and a "piece which floated a labyrinth in air, reflecting its mirrored insides in a mirror below."

17. Coplans, "Extracts from a Conversation."

Chronology

1934
Born Brian O'Doherty, Ballaghaderrin, Ireland

1939
Kidnapped briefly by gypsies

1951
Meets Thomas McGreevy

1952–56
Exhibits in *Irish Exhibition of Living Art, Royal Hibernian Academy, Exhibition of Contemporary Irish Art*

1956
Meets Jack Butler Yeats, who recommends him for a scholarship to the United States. Meets Dan Aaron, Seymour Slive. Visits New York, meets Babette Deutsch, Marianne Moore. Amazed by Museum of Modern Art.

1957
Paints last portrait of Jack Butler Yeats before his death. Receives Nuffield Fellowship grant from Cambridge University, England, to work in Experimental Psychology Laboratories; conducts research on visual perception under Alan T. Welford; sees legendary Lord Adrian bicycling through town in gaiters. Moves to United States; in September enters Harvard University School of Public Health, Cambridge, Massachusetts; works under Ross T. McFarland. Meets Barbara Novak. Lives in midst of Boston Symphony Orchestra at the home of violinist Pierre Mayer.

1958–61
Graduates with Master of Science in Hyg. from Harvard. Works at Museum of Fine Arts, Boston; while there, delivers Lowell Lectures; does television programs from galleries. Meets Edward Hopper, Marc Chagall, Walter Gropius, Josef Albers, Stuart Davis. Goes to New York City for encounter with Marcel Duchamp. Duchamp tells him we cannot tell the bather from the bathwater.

1961–64
Moves to New York City to work as an art critic for the *New York Times*. Meets Stanley Kunitz, Jack Tworkov, Bob Rauschenberg, Morton Feldman, Mark Rothko, and others. Begins making art again; first work—*The Critic's Shoes*. Starts Chess Series. Leaves the *New York Times*.

1965
Meets Eva Hesse, Dan Graham, Lucy Lippard, Sol LeWitt, Peter Hutchinson, Dorothea Rockburne, Robert Smithson, Mel Bochner, Ruth Vollmer. Shows in the *Box Show* at Byron Gallery, New York City. Begins Five Senses Series.

1966
Invites Marcel Duchamp to dinner and takes his electrocardiogram for portrait. First solo exhibition at Byron Gallery includes Five Senses, Chess, and Marcel Duchamp Series.

1967
Completes *Portrait of Marcel Duchamp*; begins Labyrinth Series. Does scenario for *Black*, a serial film; discovers Ogham (an ancient Celtic alphabet) as a serial system and makes first Ogham drawings and sculptures. Writes catalogue for Hans Richter retrospective at Finch College Museum, New York City, and exhibits there in *Schemata 7*. Composes first Structural Plays. Teaches during summer at University of California at Berkeley along with Mark Rothko and Ron Kitaj at the invitation of Peter Selz. Publishes *Object and Idea*.

1968
Finishes editing *Aspen 5/6*, a magazine in a box with records, films, and printed matter, whose contributors included Michel Butor, Roland Barthes, Susan Sontag, Mel Bochner, Sol LeWitt, Dan Graham, and others. Finishes large-scale work on categories based on research at Cambridge University.

1968–70
Continues Ogham drawings and sculptures, Structural Plays, and Vowel Choruses. Begins lifelong photographic self-portrait. Meets Joseph Cornell.

1970–72
Shows Ogham Sculptures at Betty Parsons Gallery, New York City. Continues Ogham Drawings, particularly I-Drawings. Starts Dot Drawings.

1972
Returns to Dublin; changes name to Patrick Ireland in response to Bloody Sunday in Derry, Northern Ireland. States he will sign work ''Patrick Ireland'' until such time as the British military presence is removed from Northern Ireland and all citizens are granted their civil rights. Lee Krasner tells him his name is permanent.

1973
Does first Rope Drawing at 112 Greene Street, New York City

1974
Publishes *American Masters: The Voice and the Myth* (Random House, New York), with photographs by Hans Namuth. Shows Ogham canvases at Betty Parsons Gallery.

1975
Installs *Rick* (one-half ton of peat) in Hendricks Gallery, Dublin. Jo Baer, living in Ireland, acquires the work and reports, ''It kept me warm all winter.'' Begins to superimpose multiple systems in drawings. Installs *One Drawing in Two Rooms* at Los Angeles County Museum of Art, Los Angeles, California.

1976
Begins study of Borromini's architecture in Rome. Writes series of articles, ''Inside the White Cube,'' on ideology of the gallery space for *Artforum* magazine.

1977
Ogham Drawings of the 1960s shown in *Documenta 6*, Kassel, West Germany. Traveling exhibition *Rope Drawings by Patrick Ireland* opens at the La Jolla Museum of Contemporary Art, La Jolla, California (catalogue essay by Edit deAk). Travels in Greece and Turkey studying sites, particularly Lindos, Knossus, Mycenae, Epidaurus, Ephesus.

1978
Exhibits first painted room, *Camera*, at Visual Arts Museum, New York City. Installs *A Corner for Tatlin and Fred Astaire* at Hayden Gallery, Massachusetts Institute of Technology, Cambridge.

1980
Installs *The Red Room* at Spencer Art Museum, University of Kansas, Lawrence. Jean Paul Sartre dies and memorial service is held in *The Red Room*. While at the University of Kansas gives Franklin Murphy Lectures.

1981
Installation at Fogg Art Museum, Harvard University, Cambridge, Massachusetts; *Vowel Grid* (1970) performed in courtyard (subsequent performances prohibited by Fogg administration). Installs work in Lodz, Poland; finds contrast with Soho sharply didactic.

1981–85
Continues series of Rope Drawings with painted projections in single rooms, including *Blue Room* at Butler Institute of American Art, Youngstown, Ohio, and *Kane* at Charles Cowles Gallery, New York City. Installs *Purgatory* in Hyde Gallery, Trinity College, Dublin, Ireland. Begins series of Open Box Drawings.

Catalogue

Unless otherwise stated, all works are owned by the artist and are on paper. Dimensions are given in inches; height precedes width. Asterisk (*) indicates works illustrated in catalogue.

Early Drawings

Patrick Ireland came to America from his native Ireland in 1957 to study the psychology of perception. By the mid-1960s, he had given up his theoretical studies to pursue similar interests as an artist, producing sculptures, drawings, performance works, and conceptual projects.

Ireland is interested in the various systems we have devised to plot or map space. In an early series of drawings and sculptures related to the game of chess, he took as his motif the prescribed, directional moves of the chessmen on the gridded playing board. Programmed moves on a grid also formed the basis for some ten Structural Plays that he created in the same period. In these, two players moved on two 3 x 3 floor grids, while intoning sentences that were repeated with a different word of the sentence emphasized with each repetition of the phrase. The Structural Plays, like the Chess Series, reveal the infinite possibilities of a program or system that may at first seem to be limited by its rules or structure. In the plays, language—like space—emerges as a system that permits an immense range of meaning within a highly formal construct. Ireland wrote of the Structural Plays:

The plays removed character, gesture; they flattened psychology and metaphor as the locomoted voices steamrolled their way through the dialogue. A five-word sentence could be reinhabited by five different meanings. . . . The more precise the structure, the more meanings were isolated. Thus splinted, the plasticity of language took new shapes. ("Wordless Images/Imaged Words," 1984)

In 1966–67 Patrick Ireland produced a group of flat images and motorized constructions that included and grew out of a cardiogram Ireland took of Marcel Duchamp.

Ireland's artificial oscilloscopes themselves consist of gray-painted wooden boxes of rather Minimal numbness, as much like mock-ups for real laboratory equipment as for sculpture. . . . In one of the boxes with one window the rate of the heartbeat is exaggeratedly slow, implying a protraction of body time like Duchamp's own fascination with procedures of "delay" and suggesting that because the pulsation is slowed down, Duchamp might not in this case have yet exhausted his earthly allotment of beats.

Ireland seems careful about the relation of this art to Duchamp's own; the raw heartbeat itself relates to the body as *given* in Duchamp's *Three Erotic Objects*. But the paper cardiogram is not a ready-made because it is a genuine drawing, begun at one point and moment and ended at another, drawn at two removes (machine, doctor), by the actual, if involuntary, movement of Duchamp's heart. It could be argued that it was made by two artists, but it could not be argued that it was made by no artist. . . .

In a sense the non-line of the cardiogram is a peculiarly appropriate non-signature left unwillingly behind by Duchamp's entire body, instead of a linear, cursive signature executed less polymorphously by his will through his hand. (Joseph Masheck, "On Patrick Ireland's Electrocardiographic Portrait of Marcel Duchamp," 1976)

Several of Ireland's early sculptures and drawings were based on the idea of a labyrinth, which Ireland interpreted as a confused form of space just waiting to be clarified.

I was surrounded by the labyrinth idea as a kid in Ireland, where you never get straight answers, you always get bent answers. Partly as a reaction, I suppose, I was very strong on concrete ideas and things and very much against curves. You're always slipping off curves. Also the labyrinth idea may have come from the grid of the chessboard and the paths inscribed on it by the pieces. . . .

I wanted a very clear idea of a labyrinth, like a formal garden. While in it, you could still see the whole pattern, which was complex only if you wanted to make it so. . . . It was just a few feet high, which would make you Gulliver. You could see the ways to go, but not step over. . . . All the turns were right angles, no U-turns. I clarified a motif on a St. Brigid's Cross—a kind of cartwheel that can generate an infinite system. It's very simple, but once you lost the idea you'd be lost.

Some dealt with the labyrinth as a straight line idea. Going along a straight line, with your eyes closed and turning by quarters clockwise and anticlockwise, you get lost. You've got to go on other senses. . . . I wanted to make labyrinths very easy, to diminish the urgency of a solution and to emphasize a rather lax process. . . . Mine weren't authoritarian or concerned with ''ingenuity.'' (''Janet Kardon Interviews Some Modern Maze-Makers,'' 1976)

1*
Chess Series: Bishop
1965
ink
8¾ x 10¾ in.

2
Chess Series: Wandering Knight
1965
ink
8¾ x 10¾ in.

3
Structural Play No. 2
1967
ink and typewriter
58¾ x 8½ in.

4
Scenario for Black, *A Film*
1967
ink
17 x 22 in.

5*
Portrait of Marcel Duchamp
1966
ink and typewriter on electrocardiograph form
11 x 8½ in.

6
Portrait of Marcel Duchamp: Three Leads
1966
ink and gouache
27⅝ x 35⅞ in.

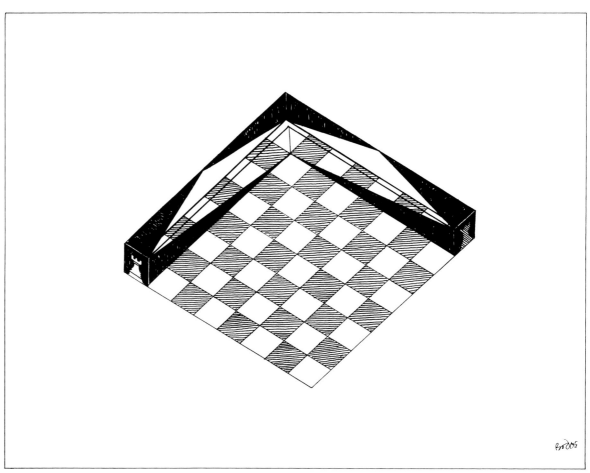

cat. no. 1

NEW YORK UNIVERSITY MEDICAL CENTER

UNIVERSITY HOSPITAL

ELECTROCARDIOGRAPH STUDY

Marcel Duchamp   4/4/'66

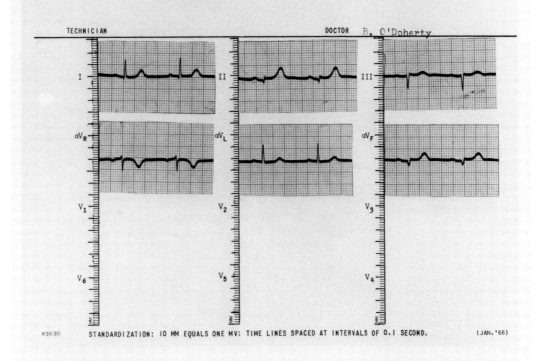

TECHNICIAN   DOCTOR   B. O'Doherty

#3630   STANDARDIZATION: 10 MM EQUALS ONE MV; TIME LINES SPACED AT INTERVALS OF 0.1 SECOND.   (JAN.'66)

cat. no. 5

7*
Portrait of Marcel Duchamp: Incremental Heartbeat
1967
ink
23 x 29 in.

8
Portrait of Marcel Duchamp: First Lead
1967
pencil
17 x 22 in.
Joseph Masheck

9*
Labyrinth
1967
gouache and colored pencils
8½ x 22 in.

10
Labyrinth as a Straight Line
1967–68
ink
18½ x 24¼ in.

11*
Study for the Five Senses: Hearing
1966
gouache, ink, and pencil
17 x 22 in.

12*
The Five Senses of the Bishop of Cloyne
1967–68
ink and watercolor
17 x 22 in.

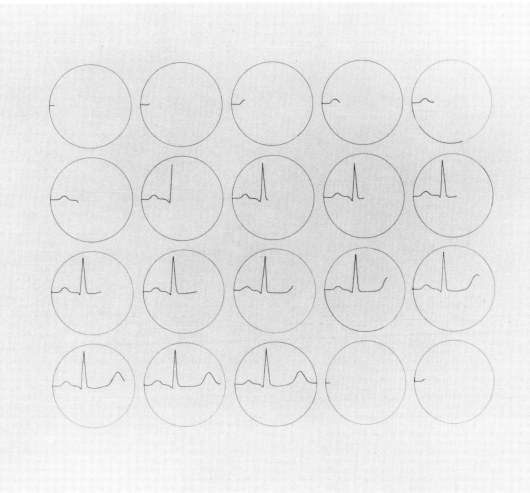

cat. no. 7

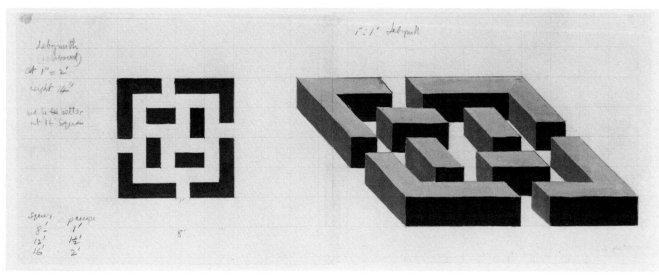

Labyrinth
(inclosed)
at 1" = 2'

height 14"

wd be better
at 16' square

1":1' Labyrinth

square	passage
8'	1'
12'	1½'
16	2'

8'

cat. no. 9

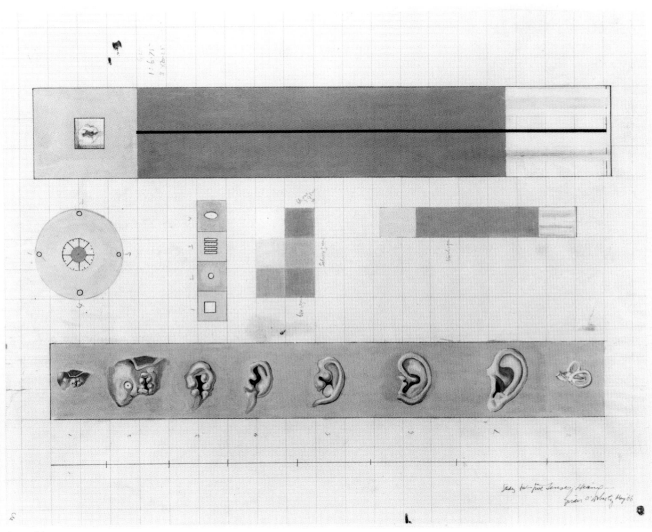

cat. no. 11

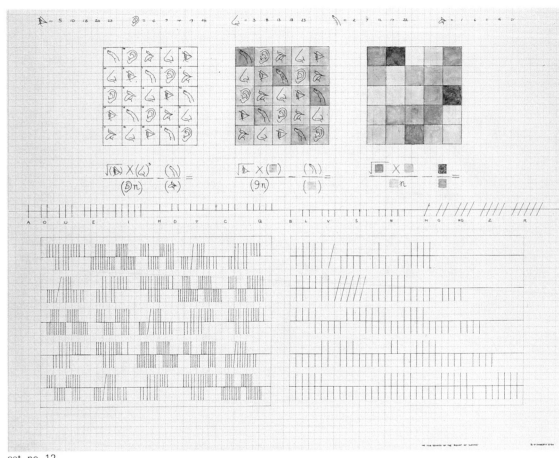

cat. no. 12

Ogham Drawings

Ireland's fascination with plotted space and structure of language led naturally to an interest in notation. He examined the alphabets and numerical systems of many cultures, in search of one that would be perfectly linear and serial. By coincidence, he found such a system in an ancient Celtic alphabet that he had first heard of as a child in Ireland. This alphabet, called Ogham (pronounced "ō-əm"), uses a horizontal centerline with groupings of short vertical or diagonal lines to distinguish the letters—letters may have from one to five vertical lines, and these may fall above, below, or across the centerline. The effect of this writing, even when viewed by those who cannot read it, is highly abstract and structured, without the more expressive qualities of the curvilinear Roman alphabet or Oriental calligraphy.

Some of Ireland's early works in Ogham are about numerical sequences; others reduce language to three words that are completely concrete and metaphysical—almost magical—in their meaning.

Back in 1967, I wanted to get three vectors crossing—the conceptual, serialism, and language. . . . For this task I boiled down my verbal culture to three words and an obsolete sign language expressed in a perfect serial system. The words were ONE. HERE. NOW. The language was Ogham, an early Christian adaption by the Celts of the Roman alphabet. ONE obviously had to do with unity, the Absolute. HERE had to do with position, thus with the ghost of composition. NOW collapsed past and future into the present. ("Wordless Images/Imaged Words," 1984)

13*
Permutations of One in a Magic Square
1967
ink
22 × 17 in.
Lucy R. Lippard

14
One to Five
1967
ink
22 × 17 in.

15*
One to Five Rotated
1967
ink
22 × 17 in.

16
One to Nine
1967
ink
22 × 17 in.

17
Study for sculpture, *Newman's Razor*
1967
ink
22 × 17 in.

18*
One Drawing
1969
colored inks
23 × 29 in.
(see page 12)

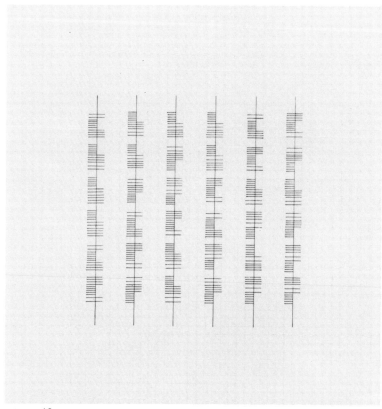

cat. no. 13

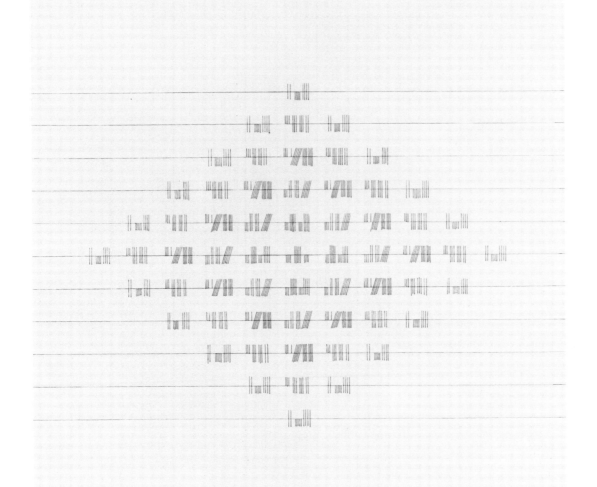

cat. no. 15

Vowel Drawings

Ireland focused his attention on the five vowels as expressed in the Ogham alphabet. In some drawings, each of the five vowels was assigned a color. In others they were stretched into straight lines, varying in length according to the number of vertical lines used to denote each in the Ogham alphabet—an A would be one unit long, while an I would be five units long. Sometimes these color- and length-coded lines would appear as grids (creating the appearance of a "Mondrian") or would break at unusual angles to create an energetic dance across the sheet.

Vowels, which are thought to be primal utterances even preceding the invention of language, represent a form of verbal communion that transcends the more specific and limited idea of communication. Several of Ireland's Vowel Drawings have been performed—intoned or even screamed by a chorus.

19
Typed Drawing
1967
typewriter and watercolor
9 × 8½ in.

20*
Vowel Chorus for Five Voices
1968
ink
17 × 22 in.
Edit deAk

21*
Vowel Lines
1968
colored inks
15½ × 16 in.

22
Black Vowels
1969
ink
22 × 30 in.

23
Vowels in Two Clusters
1971
colored inks
23 × 29 in.

24*
Vowel Grid
1969
colored inks
23 × 29 in.

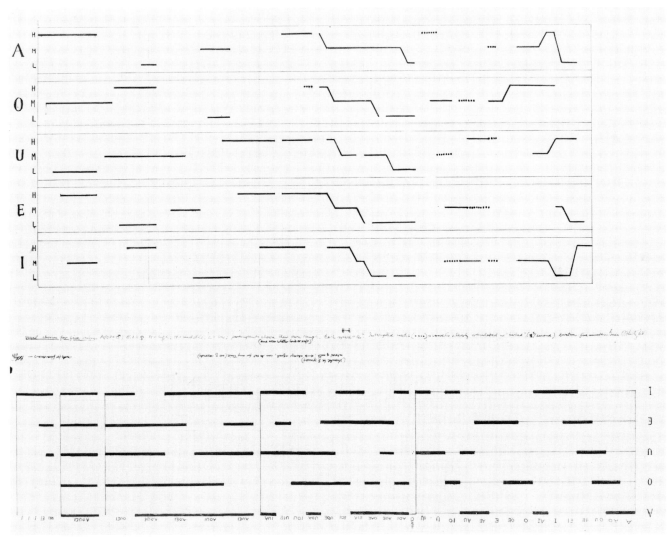

cat. no. 20

cat. no. 21

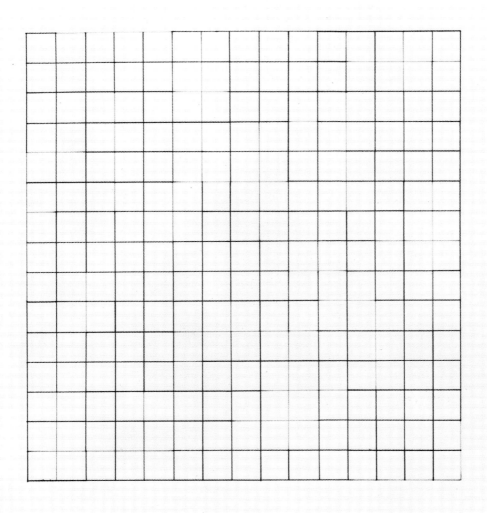

cat. no. 24

25*
Vowel Grid
1970
colored inks
23 × 29 in.

26
Vowel Square
1971
colored inks
23 × 29 in.

27
Angled Vowels
1973
colored inks
23 × 29 in.

28
Double Word-Grid
1973
colored inks
40 × 26 in.
Mr. and Mrs. Richard Koshalek, Los Angeles, California

29*
Angled Vowels at Three Scales
1975
colored inks
23 × 29 in.

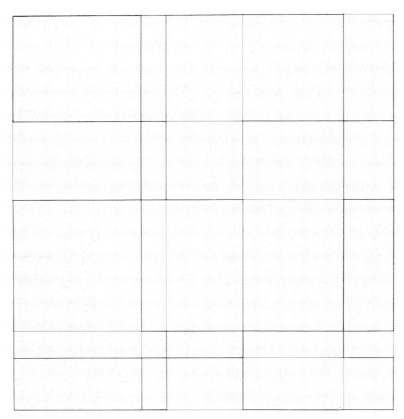

cat. no. 25

cat. no. 29

I-Drawings

Narrowing his attention still further, Ireland singled out the vowel I in a series of drawings remarkable for their formal invention. Since an I in the Ogham alphabet is written as five lines across a centerline, Ireland conceived of an I as a unit of five, which he drew variously as five dots, five wriggly lines, five straight lines (aligned or stacked), or five angled lines. These groups of five were multiplied on grids that were also based on multiples of five.

It is not without relevance that the vowel I emerged as the most intimate emblem of identity, the converse of the indefinite article A. While Ireland has consistently avoided autobiographical elements in his art, he has often explored the idea of identity as an arbitrary construction. Just as architecture is a willed structuring of space, identity may be viewed as a willed structuring of experience.

30*
375 I's
1969
colored inks
23 × 29 in.

31*
I-Drawing
1971
ink
23 × 29 in.

44

cat. no. 30

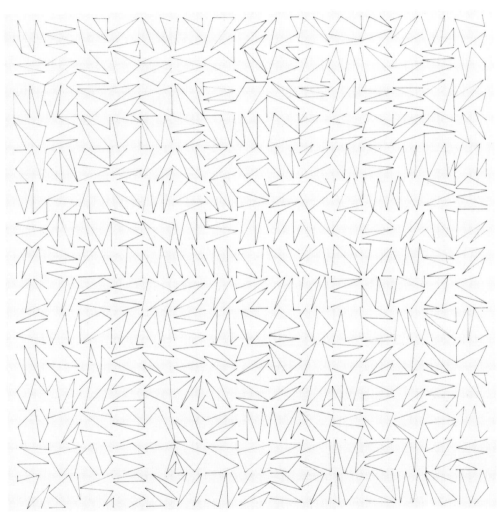

cat. no. 31

32*
I-Drawing
1972
colored inks
23 × 29 in.
Jan and Ingeborg van der Marck

33
Double I's
1973
colored inks
23 × 29 in.

34
Crossed I's
1974
colored inks
23 × 29 in.

35*
I-Drawing at Two Scales
1975
colored inks
23 × 29 in.

36*
25 Angled I's on a 5 color 5 × 5 point grid
1975
colored inks
23 × 29 in.
(cover)

37
225 I's
1972–73
colored inks on canvas
60 × 60 in.
National Museum of American Art,
Smithsonian Institution, Washington, D.C.

38
225 Large I's
1974
colored inks on canvas
60 × 60 in.

cat. no. 32

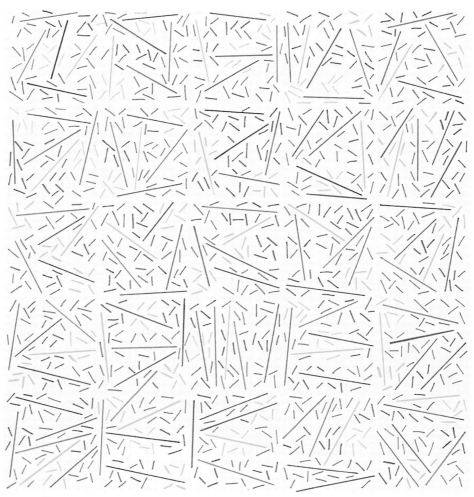

cat. no. 35

cat. no. 36

Dot Drawings

Ireland's Dot Drawings have a resonance that belies their simplicity. Just as a vowel is a primal utterance, a dot is a primary mark. Each straight line is the extension of a point, and each point implies its infinite expansion into a second or third dimension.

Several of the Dot Drawings show a dotted image, which appears again more faintly as an echo or visual remembrance. If the stronger dots carry the implication of a concrete and present reality, the fainter ones suggest the idea of history or memory. By approaching the "echo" more closely, we can strengthen its intensity. Here Ireland plays with the position of the viewer—an idea that is also crucial to the Rope Drawings, where the viewer literally walks through the drawing on a self-determined path.

Ireland has devised a means of dotting that ensures the appearance of randomness, suggesting infinite potential and a freedom from system. Yet these dots often appear within an undrawn grid, invoking the presence of a structure that may be invisible to the eye. The balance of freedom and structure, as well as present and past, emerges as a subtext.

39*
225 A's
1970
colored inks
23 × 29 in.

40
Point
1973
colored inks
23 × 29 in.

41
Image/Afterimage
1977
colored inks
23 × 29 in.

42
For Malevich, Even Though . . .
1977
colored inks
23 × 29 in.

43*
Five by Five (Aerial Perspective)
1977
colored inks
23 × 29 in.
Barbara Novak
(see page 6)

44
Image/Afterimage
1978
colored inks
23 × 29 in.

45
Point Grid
1979
ink
23 × 29 in.

cat. no. 39

Rope Installation Drawings

Like the Structural Plays, the Rope Installations that Ireland began in 1973 translate his concern for space into three dimensions while escaping the boundaries of sculpture. Most of the Rope Drawings record these temporary installations, while a few were created as studies for them.

The rope works grew out of the surprisingly optical effects of his color-coded Angled Vowel Drawings, in which reds may seem to recede and yellows appear to leap forward. Using ordinary clothesline, Ireland stretches and suspends a line within the space of a room. The participant (no longer merely an observer) moves through the room, discovering a spatial jumble from some vantage points and a clarified, architectural logic from others. Related to Ireland's early studies of perception, these Rope Installations allow ideas to be grasped empirically rather than intellectually.

Ireland has said of the Rope Installations:

Space is a kind of jungle, a complete chaos with no rhyme or reason at all. The ropes draw temporary propositions that give brief visions of order. But that order is always lapsing into chaos again, with each new step. For the pieces change radically with even small moves. Thus they are to a degree unknowable—there is no single gestalt, just a succession of order and disorder. Eventually both of these conceptions proceed from the mind—the piece enables you to make your own disorder or order. There is no one right view. (Quoted in Dorothy Walker, *Patrick Ireland*, 1985)

Ireland sometimes takes his inspiration for the Rope Installations and the drawings that record or prepare them from favorite spatial constructs, such as Tatlin's sculpture, Matisse's still-life interiors, Borromini's architecture, Rimbaud's poem on vowels, Joyce's opening to *Finnegan's Wake*, and the Vatican *stanze*.

46
Corner for Tatlin and Fred Astair
Rope Drawing #54 at the Hayden Gallery,
Massachusetts Institute of Technology, Cambridge
1979
colored inks
26 × 40 in.
Atlantic Richfield Corporate Art Collection

47*
The Red Room
Rope Drawing #57 at the Spencer Art Museum,
University of Kansas, Lawrence
1980
red ink
26 × 40 in.
Spencer Museum of Art, University of Kansas,
Lawrence; Gift of Mrs. Paul Ward

48
Borromini's Underpass
Rope Drawing #58 at the Akron Art Museum,
Akron, Ohio
1980
ink
26 × 40 in.
Charles Cowles Gallery, New York

49
String Quartet (4 Corners)
Rope Drawing #65 at the Brooklyn Museum of Art, New York
1983
colored inks
26 × 40 in.
Charles Cowles Gallery, New York

50*
Rimbaud's Cradle
Rope Drawing #70 at the Charles Cowles Gallery, New York
1983
colored inks
26 × 40 in.
Private collection, Courtesy Charles Cowles Gallery,
New York

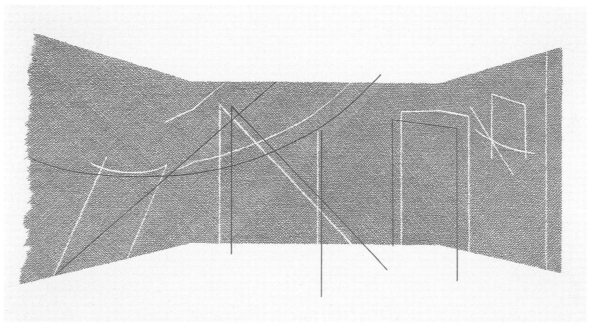

cat. no. 47

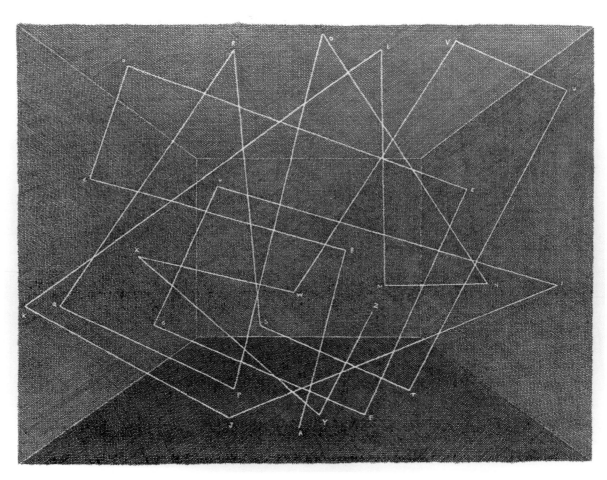

cat. no. 50

51
Drawing for *Big A*
Rope Drawing #72 at the University of Virginia,
Charlottesville
1984
colored inks
26 × 40 in.
Charles Cowles Gallery, New York

52
Study for *Purgatory*
Rope Drawing #74 at the Hyde Gallery,
Trinity College, Dublin
1985
ink
26 × 40 in.
Charles Cowles Gallery, New York

53*
Study for *Purgatory, Four Spatial #56/Verbal Propositions*
Rope Drawing #74 at the Hyde Gallery,
Trinity College, Dublin
1985
colored inks
26 × 40 in.
Charles Cowles Gallery, New York

54*
Study for *Purgatory*
Rope Drawing #74 at the Hyde Gallery,
Trinity College, Dublin
1985
ink
26 × 40 in.
Charles Cowles Gallery, New York

56

cat. no. 53

cat. no. 54

Planes and Boxes

In a group of drawings of closed and open boxes, Ireland continues the spatial plays of such Rope Installations as *String Quartet* (in which the four corners of a room were made to "disappear," straightening out an angled space). Closed forms dissolve in transparent planes or explode in many directions, confounding notions of inside and outside. The cube or rectangular box found in these drawings seems an idealized or abstracted evocation of the contemporary artist's gallery space, which Ireland (under his given name, Brian O'Doherty) discussed in detail in a series of articles entitled "Inside the White Cube," published in *Artforum* in 1976.

The latest drawings show a new awareness of draftsmanship in their concentrated cross-hatching. The visual beauty of line and color were apparent in Ireland's drawings as early as his Vowel Drawings of the late 1960s and early 1970s, but emerge as more independent elements in the Open Boxes.

55*
36 Lines in 6 Planes
1977
colored inks
23 × 29 in.

56*
Twelve Planes
1978
pencil
23 × 29 in.

57*
Open Box (blue background)
1985
colored inks
23 × 29 in.
Julius S. Held

58
Open Box (green background)
1985
colored inks
23 × 29 in.

59
Open Boxes (gray background)
1985
colored inks
23 × 29 in.

cat. no. 55

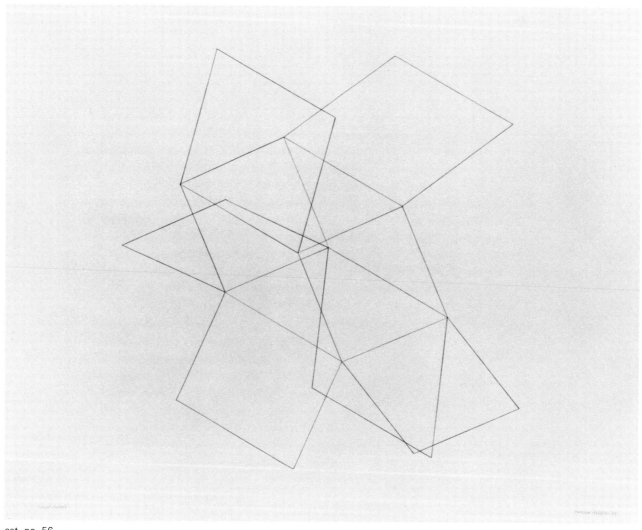

cat. no. 56

cat. no. 57

Selected Bibliography

62

Asterisk (*) denotes those publications for which the artist provided a statement or an interview.

Baker, Kenneth. "Patrick Ireland: Limits of the Eye." *Art in America* 72 (Summer 1984): 130–33.

Bowles, Jerry C. "Brian O'Doherty Whispers in Ogham." *Art News* 69 (September 1970): 34–35 ff.

Brown, Christopher. "The Equivocal Art of Patrick Ireland." *Artweek* 10 (June 16, 1979): 3.

*Coplans, John. "Extracts from a Conversation Between John Coplans and Patrick Ireland." *Dialogue* (May–June 1980): 4–7.

*DeAk, Edit. *Rope Drawings by Patrick Ireland*. La Jolla, California: La Jolla Museum of Contemporary Art, 1977.

*Foote, Nancy. "Situation Esthetics: Impermanent Art and the Seventies Audience." *Artforum* 18 (January 1980): 27.

Foster, Hal. "Patrick Ireland." *Artforum* 19 (November 1980): 84.

Fox, Howard. "The Thorny Issues of Temporary Art." *Museum News* 57 (July–August 1979): 42–50.

Goodman, Sherry. "Patrick Ireland." *Arts Magazine* 57 (October 1982): 12.

*Ireland, Patrick (as Brian O'Doherty). "Minus Plato." *Art and Artists* 1 (September 1966): 10–11. Reprinted in *Minimal Art: A Critical Anthology*, ed. by Gregory Battcock, New York: E. P. Dutton, Inc., 1968, 372–74.

*_____ . "Wordless Images/Imaged Words." *Poetry East* 13/14 (Spring/Summer 1984): 164–66.

Jeppson, Gabriella. *Patrick Ireland*. Cambridge: Fogg Art Museum, 1981.

*Kardon, Janet. "Janet Kardon Interviews Some Modern Mazemakers." *Art International* 20 (April–May 1976): 64–68.

Lippard, Lucy R. *Overlay: Contemporary Art and the Art of Prehistory*. New York: Pantheon Books, 1983, 88–89.

Masheck, Joseph. *The Duchamp Portrait 1966/67*. Washington, D.C.: The Corcoran Gallery of Art, 1974. Reprinted and slightly expanded as "Patrick Ireland's Electrocardiographic Portrait of Marcel Duchamp," *Arts Magazine* 51 (May 1976): 108–09.

*McCabe, Cynthia. *The Golden Door: Artist-Immigrants of America*. Washington, D.C.: Smithsonian Institution Press for the Hirshhorn Museum and Sculpture Garden, 1976, 377–78.

O'Doherty, Brian. See Ireland, Patrick.

Onorato, Ronald. "The Modern Maze." *Art International* 20 (April–May 1976): 21–25.

Preisman, Fran. "Patrick Ireland's Rope Drawings." *Artweek* 8 (March 12, 1977): 1, 20.

*Varian, Elayne H. "Interview with Brian O'Doherty." *Schemata 7*. New York: Finch College Museum of Art, 1967.

*_____ . "Interview with Brian O'Doherty." *Art International* 14 (December 1970): 30–33.

Walker, Dorothy. "Installations and Performance in Ireland." *Flash Art* 92–93 (October–November 1979): 39–41.

*_____ . *Patrick Ireland*. Dublin: Douglas Hyde Gallery, Trinity College, 1985.

Lenders to the Exhibition

Anonymous lender, courtesy Charles Cowles Gallery, New York
Atlantic Richfield Corporate Art Collection
Charles Cowles Gallery, New York
Edit deAk
Julius S. Held
Patrick Ireland
Mr. and Mrs. Richard Koshalek, Los Angeles, California
Lucy R. Lippard
Jan and Ingeborg van der Marck
Joseph Masheck
National Museum of American Art, Smithsonian Institution
Barbara Novak
Spencer Museum of Art, University of Kansas, Lawrence